LAURA INGALLS WILDER

Essential Lives

LAURA INGALLS WILDER

BY EMMA CARLSON BERNE

Content Consultant
Nicole Elzenga
Collections Manager
Laura Ingalls Wilder Museum
Walnut Grove, Minnesota

ABDO
Publishing Company

CREDITS

Published by ABDO Publishing Company, 8000 West 78th Street, Edina, Minnesota 55439. Copyright © 2008 by Abdo Consulting Group, Inc. International copyrights reserved in all countries. No part of this book may be reproduced in any form without written permission from the publisher. The Essential Library™ is a trademark and logo of ABDO Publishing Company.

Printed in the United States.

Editor: Rebecca Rowell
Cover Design: Becky Daum
Interior Design: Lindaanne Donohoe

Library of Congress Cataloging-in-Publication Data
Berne, Emma Carlson.
  Laura Ingalls Wilder / Emma Carlson Berne.
    p. cm. . — (Essential lives)
  Includes bibliographical references and index.
  ISBN-13: 978-1-59928-843-7
I. Wilder, Laura Ingalls, 1867–1957—Juvenile literature. 2. Women authors, American—20th century—Biography—Juvenile literature. 3. Women pioneers—United States—Biography—Juvenile literature. 4. Frontier and pioneer life—United States—Juvenile literature. 5. Children's stories—Authorship—Juvenile literature. [I. Wilder, Laura Ingalls, 1867–1957.] I. Title.

PS3545.I342Z5695 2007
813'.52—dc22 [B]

                                                    2007012513

TABLE OF CONTENTS

Laura and Almanzo Wilder's house on Rocky Ridge Farm

THE BOOK NO
DEPRESSION COULD STOP

The end of 1929 was the beginning of a difficult time for America. The stock market crash created problems for companies and individuals nationwide. Banks failed, which caused millions of families to lose all of their savings and investments.

Businesses closed. People lost their jobs and then their houses. The Great Depression had begun.

Rocky Ridge Farm outside of Mansfield, Missouri, was peaceful and beautiful. The fields were neatly plowed and planted. The garden was bursting with pumpkins, lettuce, beans, and radishes. White curtains fluttered at the windows of the sprawling white frame house. Its foundation was built with stones from the creek on the property. The lovely farm was the result of 36 years of hard work and careful saving, but it was not immune to the Great Depression ravaging the country.

Inside the farm's tidy kitchen stood a white-haired woman with big eyes so blue they were almost violet. She was 62 years old and only five feet (1.5 m) tall. Her name was Laura Ingalls Wilder. This was the Laura Ingalls who was born in a little log cabin in Wisconsin and who later married Almanzo Wilder in South Dakota. This was the Laura Ingalls Wilder who told the stories of her family's adventures traveling by covered wagon across the country. She was the Laura Ingalls Wilder who would become one of the most famous and beloved children's authors in the world.

Read Globally

The Little House books have global appeal. They have been translated into a few dozen languages so readers worldwide may enjoy them.

Right now, Laura was just worried. She had recently received word that a brokerage firm in which she had some stocks had lost all of its investments in the stock market crash. Laura and her husband, Almanzo, had a comfortable life, but they had no money to spare. A few years before, at the urging of their daughter, Rose, Laura and Almanzo had scraped together some savings and invested in stocks.

Rose also lived on the farm, but in a different house over a little hill. Rose was a popular writer. She wrote books, stories, and magazine articles. When she heard about the loss of Laura and Almanzo's stocks, Rose started worrying about her parents. They were getting old. She wondered how they would survive through their old age without money. Rose was their only child. She loved her parents but did not want to be stuck at home taking care of them.

Rose loved to travel. She had lived in different places around the world: Albania, Turkey, Egypt, and France. She had many international friends

"Pioneer Girl"

Laura actually wrote her autobiography before she and Rose worked on the story "When Grandma Was a Little Girl." Laura wrote "Pioneer Girl" during the early part of 1930. Rose showed the manuscript to her literary agent and a few editors, but no one wanted to publish it. When Marion Fiery asked for a longer version of "When Grandma Was a Little Girl," Rose offered her "Pioneer Girl." Fiery did not like the book. Few people have heard of "Pioneer Girl" because it was never published.

and longed to see them again. She was 42 years old, and the thought of staying on the farm for the rest of her life to provide for her parents made Rose feel like she was being smothered. There had to be a way for them to make some money.

Laura had always told stories about her childhood. Rose had grown up hearing them. For years, Laura had written for a farm newspaper called the *Missouri Ruralist*. She often included memories of the prairies in her column. From her two decades as a writer, Rose knew good money could be made from stories. Even though times were bad for the country, including the publishing industry, Rose thought her mother could make a little money from her memoirs.

Rose proposed the idea to her mother. Perhaps Laura could turn some of the little vignettes she had written for her newspaper column into a book. Rose would help—she knew all about writing and editing. Laura was intrigued. Readers of her column had always seemed to enjoy hearing about her childhood memories. Plus, Laura had been interested for some time in writing her life story. She agreed to do it.

Working as a team, Laura and Rose created a 20-page story called "When Grandma Was a Little Girl." It was the story of Laura's growing up in Wisconsin.

Laura included many of the tales her father had told her of his adventures growing up. The story was created as a picture book. When it was done, Rose gave the manuscript to Berta Hader, a writer friend. Hader had written a lot of children's books. She thought the story was good, so she passed it on to an editor named Marion Fiery. Fiery was head of children's publishing at Alfred Knopf, a big publisher in New York City.

Changing the Title

The title *House in the Big Woods* was chosen by Laura's first publisher, Knopf. When the book was later produced by Harper and Brothers, the publisher added the word *Little* to balance out the word *Big,* making the title *Little House in the Big Woods.*

Fiery liked the book. There was something about it that captured her attention. The story was of a family working together and using traditional farming skills. Laura's words gave a sense of joy and optimism—two things that were much needed during the Depression. However, the manuscript would need a lot of work before it could be published.

Fiery returned the manuscript to Laura. She wanted Laura to expand the story into a chapter book for older children. Fiery wanted more detail, including descriptions of farm activities such as butchering, harvesting crops, churning butter, making bread—all of the tasks Laura and her family spent their lives doing.

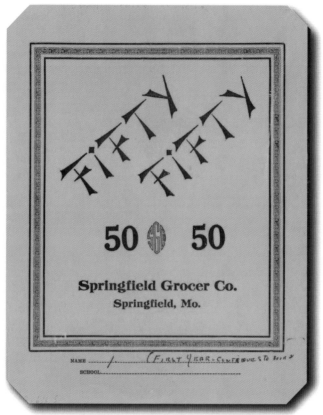

Laura Ingalls Wilder wrote her stories in pencil on five-cent tablets.

Laura got to work revising the manuscript. For two months, she sat in her little corner study in her farmhouse and wrote in longhand on orange-covered school tablets. She plumbed her memory for all the details of the way her mother used to color butter using scraped carrots and the delicious aroma of a pig's tail roasting over the fire after a hog was butchered. Laura thought of her sister Mary's beautiful golden curls and the pumpkins and squashes in the attic during winter. She wrote down all the details of her father's stories of panthers and bears in the woods. When Laura finished, Rose sent off the revised manuscript to Fiery. Laura and Rose waited nervously for a response.

A month later, Fiery wrote back. Knopf loved the book. The publishers wanted to call it *House in the Big Woods*. With Laura's approval, they were going to move ahead with production.

Rose and Laura were jubilant—Laura was going to be published! But their joy did not last long. A short time later, Fiery wrote to Laura with the bad news that Knopf was closing its children's department. Declining book sales meant they could not afford to keep it open. Fiery was losing her job. Laura's book would not get the attention it deserved or would need to sell well.

For a brief period, it seemed that Laura and Rose's efforts had failed. But Fiery believed in Laura's book. No one knows for certain, but it was

Virginia Kirkus

Virginia Kirkus was the chief editor of children's books for Harper and Brothers from 1925 to 1932. This was a time when most American women did not even attend college, much less have careers outside the home. Kirkus had a reputation for finding sleepers, which are now-famous books that might otherwise have been overlooked. She founded *Kirkus Reviews,* one of America's leading book review journals. The publication is still in circulation today.

Laura Ingalls Wilder at age 62

probably through Fiery that the manuscript landed on the desk of Virginia Kirkus at the publishing house Harper and Brothers. Kirkus also liked the manuscript, writing of Laura, "The real magic was in the telling. One felt that one was listening, not reading."[1]

Kirkus's experience with Laura's books would one day be the same for millions of children. Kirkus realized that she was holding in her hands "the book no depression could stop."[2] Laura's writing was at the same time simple and inspiring, exciting and soothing.

More than that, Laura's stories depicted many of the values people worried were being lost with progress: families working together, simple farming methods, and preservation of stories of old times.

On November 26, 1931, Laura received a telegram with the news that Harper and Brothers had accepted her manuscript. Though she had no idea at the time, Laura was about to embark on a great adventure. At age 62, she had long assumed her adventuring was done. She had lived through many difficult situations, including blizzards, near-starvation, fires, and grasshopper plagues. This time, her adventure would come in the telling of all the exciting stories from her youth.

Writing in Middle Age

Laura Ingalls Wilder wrote about her childhood and becoming an author later in life, noting, "Children today could not have a childhood like mine in the Big Woods of Wisconsin, but they could learn of it and hear the stories Pa used to tell. But I put off writing them from year to year and was past 60 when I wrote my first book, *The Little House in the Big Woods.*"[3]

By the time she was finished, Laura Ingalls Wilder would publish eight books that would sell millions of copies and remain in print for more than 75 years. She would become an icon to generations of readers. But that was all in the future. Laura Ingalls Wilder's story begins decades earlier, in the woods of Wisconsin.

Laura wrote her Little House stories at home at this desk.

Charles and Caroline Ingalls, Laura's parents

BORN IN THE DEEP WOODS

aura Ingalls's life started in an area of Wisconsin known as the "Big Woods." When Laura was very little, the Big Woods seemed to stretch on forever. In a way, she was right. Wisconsin in the 1800s was a remote and beautiful place. The woods were full of 100-year-old oak, elm, and ash trees barely touched by loggers. Though settlers had moved in, black bears, wolves, and wild cats still roamed freely. These large predators fed on the deer, wild pigs, rabbits, and squirrels that inhabited the woods.

In a little log cabin on a small farm at the edge of these woods, Laura Elizabeth Ingalls was born February 7, 1867, to Charles and Caroline Ingalls. Laura was the couple's second child.

Charles and Caroline already had a little girl. Laura's older sister, Mary, had been born two years earlier. Mary had beautiful golden curls. Baby Laura looked just like her father. She had his wild brown hair and sparkling blue eyes.

That was likely a happy winter for the young family. They stayed inside together. No one went out much during the winter because the world outside was icy and cold. The snow was in drifts almost as high as the cabin's roof. The temperature was probably well below zero. All of the wild animals were snuggled in their dens.

There were no crops or garden to tend. Sometimes, Charles would go hunting. Mostly, though, the Ingalls family was cozy in their tiny log

The Big Woods

There is more than one Big Woods in the Upper Midwest. Minnesota and Wisconsin both have a Big Woods. Laura lived in the Big Woods of Wisconsin.

cabin. The snow provided insulation from the cold
outside and a good fire in the hearth kept the house
warm. Charles greased his traps for mink, muskrat,
and bear. Caroline sewed, cooked, and cleaned. Mary
played on the floor as baby Laura slept in her cradle.

Even though they lived in the woods, the Ingalls
family was neither lonely nor isolated. Their cabin was
seven miles (11 km) from the town of Pepin. Laura's
grandparents, aunts, uncles, and cousins all lived a
short drive away by sleigh or wagon.

Charles's parents, Laura's grandparents, lived in a
big cabin a little farther down the road. Their names
were Lansford and Laura. Baby Laura was named after
her grandmother.

Pepin, Wisconsin

The town of Pepin,
Wisconsin, thrives today.
The woods have long
been cut down, but a
replica of the Ingalls
family cabin was built
where the original cabin
once stood. In addition,
the town holds an annual
Laura Ingalls Wilder Days
festival.

Lansford and Laura Ingalls
had not always lived in Wisconsin.
Charles was born in New York
in 1836. He was the third of
ten children. Charles always
remembered that he had a happy
childhood growing up on his
parents' farm, with plenty of
adventures that he would later tell
to his daughters. When he was a boy,
Charles's family moved from the

woods of New York to the prairies of Illinois. It was perhaps there that Charles first fell in love with open grasslands and big sky—a love he would pass on to Laura. Lansford and Laura Ingalls struggled to support their large family, however, and soon decided their luck would be better in newly settled Jefferson County, Wisconsin. In 1853, when Charles was 17, the entire family packed up again and moved to the Big Woods.

Waiting to Marry

Caroline Ingalls would have been considered an older bride when she married Charles at 21. Women in the 1800s often married in their late teens. Some girls married as early as 13, though that was rare. Laura was 18 when she married Almanzo Wilder—a more typical age for her era.

Lansford and Laura bought land down the road from the farm of Charlotte Quiner, a widow with seven children. Her husband had died many years before. The family did not have much money. Charlotte would have depended a great deal on her oldest daughter, 14-year-old Caroline, to help take care of the house and the younger children.

The arrival of the Ingalls family must have been exciting for the Quiners and a welcome change from the hard work of the farm. Because their children were the same age, the two families started visiting. Caroline spent time with Charles, who undoubtedly charmed her with his laughter and merry tunes on the fiddle.

Eventually, three pairs of Quiner and Ingalls children would marry, including Charles and Caroline in 1860. When they wed, Charles was 24 and Caroline was 21.

Jefferson County did not provide the better life the Ingalls had hoped it would. Not only was the area crowded, but the county was gripped in an economic depression that had begun a few years earlier. When Lansford lost the title to his land in 1862 because he could not pay the mortgage, the entire Ingalls clan—including newlyweds Charles and Caroline—moved northwest to Pepin County. Pepin was at the very edge of the Big Woods.

Panthers

In *Little House in the Big Woods*, Laura tells several stories of panthers. She writes of them living in treetops, waiting to drop down on prey. Laura describes the cats as big enough to kill a horse. The cat Laura describes is actually a puma, or cougar. Cougars are no longer found in Wisconsin due to destruction of their habitat. However, a few still live in the wild in the lower third of the United States.

Cougars can weigh up to 200 pounds (91 kg). They are excellent hunters, runners, and climbers. They even swim. They usually eat deer and other animals of a similar size. The name *panther* is the common term for leopards or jaguars that have a black coat. These animals are found in Asia.

Laura's description of panthers is confusing because she writes of the cats of Wisconsin as black. The cougars of North America are typically tawny-colored, with black-tipped ears and tails and a white belly. Black cougars have never existed in North America, but stories of them have circulated since the 1600s. Experts believe such sightings were probably due to reflections from light or tricks of the eye since these animals were usually spotted at night.

Charles and Henry Quiner, his brother-in-law, purchased 80 acres (32 ha) of land near the town of Pepin, divided it in half, and settled down to farm.

In some ways, life in the Big Woods was easy. The woods were full of deer and rabbits that were hunted for food. Their skins were made into shoes and hats. Mink, muskrat, and foxes were trapped for their fur, which could be traded in town for flour, cornmeal, and sugar. Lake Pepin, a wide part of the Mississippi River, was an abundant source of fresh fish, ducks, and geese.

Farming was a never-ending cycle of labor. Clearing a tiny patch of land for planting crops meant cutting down huge trees. Once cut down, the trees had to be split into logs and hauled away. Their giant stumps had to be pried from the ground. Charles and his fellow settlers did all of this work with axes, saws, and horses. After the land was cleared, there was endless hoeing and pulling of the saplings that sprouted everywhere. More and more, Charles thought of the open grasslands he

Western Land

One Laura Ingalls Wilder scholar, Donald Zochert, has speculated that Charles may have gotten the idea to move west from a newspaper ad. During the 1860s, the Union Pacific Railroad wrote an ad that read, "Kansas Farms! Neosho Valley Lands. 1,300,000 Acres for Sale to Actual Settlers."[1]

had seen in Illinois. Travelers and newspapers brought word of land available in Kansas and Missouri—places without trees as far as the horizon. The economy was suffering from yet another depression. Charles had to provide for his wife and daughters. Perhaps it was time to say goodbye to Wisconsin.

Charles and Caroline discussed the matter. Henry and Polly Quiner discussed the matter. Both couples decided they would leave Wisconsin.

In 1868, Charles and Henry hitched their horses to their covered wagons. Baby Laura and four-year-old Mary were carefully tucked into the back of the wagon along with all of Charles and Caroline's belongings: bedding, pots, clothes, shoes, flour, cornmeal, salt pork, and coffee—everything they would need. The two families pulled out on the road and headed west.

Leaving Family

Charles and Caroline Ingalls took a big risk when they left their families in Wisconsin. The support of relatives was very important for settlers. Many farm tasks required several people. Families often worked together to build houses, butcher animals, pickle the fruits and vegetables from their gardens, and make cheese.

During their many travels by covered wagon, the Ingalls family
would have stopped to make dinner and camp for the night.

*After the Civil War, pioneers flooded the Great Plains,
hoping to homestead the prairies.*

Discovering the Prairie

The Ingalls and Quiner families headed west in their wagons, planning to settle in Missouri. While still in the Big Woods, they had purchased a farm of 160 acres (64 ha) from a land dealer named Adamantine Johnson. The families were going to split the land.

The two families were not the only people who thought Missouri and Kansas would be good places to settle. That area of the country long had been the home of many Native American tribes. For years, the federal government battled the tribes for possession of the land, all the while fighting the Civil War. Once the war was over, the government focused on conquering the tribes of Native Americans. The land was opened up for settlement in the late 1860s. People flooded the country in a massive wave, looking to start farms. The Ingalls and Quiner families were in the midst of this migration.

The two families made their way to Missouri in 1869, but their stay was brief—at least long enough to sign a legal document. No one really knows why they did not stay. Whatever happened, Henry and Polly Quiner went back to the Big Woods in 1870. Alone with their two small children, Charles and Caroline Ingalls headed across the prairie toward Kansas.

Locating the Little House

Laura writes in *Little House on the Prairie* that her family's homestead site was 40 miles (64 km) from the town of Independence, Kansas. Historians agree that the Ingalls family lived only 13 miles (21 km) from the town, near the Verdigris River. Laura may have gotten the distance wrong when she gathered facts from relatives, or she may have deliberately altered the distance to enhance the sense of isolation the family felt on the prairie.

In her books, Laura recalls journeys by covered wagon fondly. In truth, traveling by wagon was difficult. Progress was very slow because the wagon only went about two miles per hour (3 km/h). Out on the open prairie, there was almost no protection from the wind, rain, and cold. The wheels were made of wood rimmed with iron and had no shocks. This made the wagon ride very bumpy and uncomfortable.

In addition to simply being uncomfortable, the journey was dangerous. Like any newly settled area, the region had many criminals who came to take advantage of the limited law enforcement and vulnerable pioneers.

The Osage Tribe

The Native Americans Laura and her family encountered in Kansas belonged to the Osage tribe. Before settlers entered the area, the Osage lived and hunted on a huge area of land bordered by four rivers: the Missouri, the Mississippi, the Arkansas, and the Osage. By the time the Ingalls family arrived, the tribe was living on the federally designated Osage Indian Reservation. The reservation was located on a small section of land at the extreme west of the tribe's original grounds, which they had occupied for hundreds of years.

Though they planted a variety of crops, the Osage were primarily hunters. Three times a year, the entire tribe left their villages on the riverbanks for their annual hunts on the plains. These were large-scale events that required a great deal of planning.

People who encountered the Osage often remarked on their height—many men were well over 6 feet tall (2 m)—and well-dressed appearance. They shaved their hair into scalplocks that they decorated with string and feathers. Many adults had pierced ears from which they hung elaborate earrings.

Charles and Caroline must have worried about roadside bandits waiting to rob wagons. Caroline had another worry—she was pregnant again. Taking care of two little girls, enduring a bumpy wagon ride for several hours a day, and camping on rough land miles from a doctor must have been hard for her.

Space for settlement in Kansas was plentiful. Most of the Native Americans who originally lived there

Birth and Death

Caroline Ingalls was a lucky woman. She lived through six pregnancies and deliveries. Many women were not as fortunate. For women in the 1800s, childbirth was the number one cause of death. Frontier women, who frequently gave birth in crude shelters far from midwives and doctors, often fared the worst.

had been killed or driven away. There were only a few areas left as reservations for remaining tribes, including the Osage Indian Reservation, a 50-mile-wide (80 km) stretch of land across the southern part of Kansas. The federal government had set aside this land for the Osage after pushing them off their original tribal home along the Osage River in Missouri.

For unknown reasons, many settlers decided to build their farms on the reservation, including Charles and Caroline. Charles built the family's cabin next to an active Native American trail that he mistakenly thought was no longer in use. Charles was concerned for his family. Caroline and the girls needed shelter.

With the help of his neighbors, Charles built a log cabin from trees he cut down in the creek bottom. He began breaking the tough sod for crops, built a stable, and dug a well. Caroline continued her never-ending tasks of laundry, cooking, and cleaning. She also helped Charles and started a garden—an important source of food for the family.

One day, Charles took a break from his work. He, Laura, and Mary went to explore an abandoned Osage campsite near their home. It was rare for any farmer to take a day off from work in the middle of the week, but Charles and the girls needed to give Caroline some privacy. When they returned home that evening, there was a new baby tucked into the bed beside Caroline. A third daughter had been born. Her name was also Caroline, but no one ever called her anything but Carrie.

The Family Hog

Laura writes extensively of hog butchering in *Little House in the Big Woods.* Hog butchering was an important time for most rural families in the 1800s. The family hog was a major food source. The hog would be carefully fattened on table scraps throughout the year and then slaughtered once it was cold enough to keep the meat frozen. Every part of the hog was used, even the bristles and head.

Life was not peaceful on the prairie. Tensions between the settlers and the Osage were high. Many families moved onto the reservation. Federal soldiers made a few weak attempts to discourage settlers from trespassing.

The Osage began holding war councils in the creek bottoms. There was increased traffic by Native Americans on the trail running by the Ingalls house. Everyone feared there would be attacks.

A Home on the Prairie
The little log cabin Charles built in Kansas has long been lost to the sun and rain of the prairies. A replica of the house has been built for visitors to enjoy.

It was too much stress for Charles and Caroline. How could they raise their three daughters and make a home in this dangerous place? Moreover, Charles had gotten word that federal soldiers were going to remove the people from their farms—and this time, they meant it. In 1870, the man to whom Charles had sold his Wisconsin farm wrote and said he was no longer able to make payments on it. He asked Charles to buy back the farm. Charles and Caroline decided to accept his offer.

The couple promptly packed the wagon again and left the log house Charles had built. The family began the long trip back to Wisconsin. When Charles, Caroline, and the girls finally arrived at the Big Woods, their families welcomed them back to their same little cabin. They had been gone for three years.

Laura was four years old when the family settled back into life in the Big Woods. She later described this period in her life vividly in *Little House in the Big Woods*.

Even though Laura was still so young, she and Mary would help Caroline around the house. They had to make their bed and pick up wood chips to start a fire. They watched Caroline at butchering time as she smoked hams, pickled pork shoulder, and ground sausage. Caroline made cheese and butter from the family cow's milk. She boiled the laundry in a giant kettle on the stove or in the yard and then hung it on clotheslines. Caroline weeded the garden. Early on, Laura and Mary learned that pioneer women always had work to do.

Laura remembered her mother as a quiet, steady woman who taught her daughters everything they would need to know to be good wives and mothers. She remembered her father as a magical man who played games, told stories, and played his fiddle. Laura wrote when she was an old woman,

> *Years ago, in the little house in the Big Woods, Sister Mary and I listened to father's stories … when the day's work was done, we sat in the twilight or by the evening lamp and listened to Pa's stories and the music of his violin … Mary and I loved Pa's stories best. We never forgot them.*[1]

The log cabin in the Big Woods was a happy place to grow up. ⌒

Above:
Charles Ingalls, Laura's father
Left: Laura Ingalls Wilder had many fond memories of Pa playing his fiddle.

Homesteaders on the Great Plains often lived in sod houses.

ADVENTURES ON
PLUM CREEK

Though growing crops in the Big Woods was difficult because of all the trees, making a living there was not challenging. Once a farmer cleared his field, he could plant with relative ease. In addition to farming, there was plenty of game and fish for hunting, trapping, and fishing. The family had a cow for milk and butter and a garden for vegetables. It was a pleasant life.

But the country was becoming crowded. As westward expansion continued, more and more people moved into the area. Charles did not like being so close to neighbors. More than that, he liked adventure and travel. Caroline, on the other hand, enjoyed being around people. Laura agreed with her father. She liked wild places and adventures.

The country was in the midst of a great wave of movement from east to west. Charles wanted to join it. In the winter of 1873, Charles and Caroline sold their property to a new settler for $1,000. The Ingalls family packed its belongings and drove through the deep snow and ice to Charles's parents' big cabin. The family needed time to prepare for the journey west. Charles's brother Peter and his wife, Eliza, were going with them part of the way. The couple had already rented a farm in another part of Wisconsin.

The Railroad

During the 1870s and 1880s, the country was in a fever to complete the transcontinental railroad, which would eventually stretch to the East Coast, opening the western frontier for settlement. This was the railroad that the Ingalls family lived by in Walnut Grove, Minnesota. A decade later, they would live near the same line in De Smet, South Dakota.

Before the families could leave, however, the children came down with scarlet fever. This dangerous illness could cause brain damage or even death. The adults were anxious. They were worried about the children. To make matters worse, it looked as if the trip might have to wait an entire year. The families had to cross the Mississippi River before the ice broke, and it was growing thin.

The children recovered in time to make the trip across the Mississippi. As soon as the children were well enough to travel, the wagons were packed. The families could not waste a single day more. The goodbyes were

Sod Houses

The first thing pioneers on the prairies needed were shelters from the endless winds and rainstorms that frequently pelted the region. Wood was scarce on the plains, so many settlers built sod houses. These could be dug into a bank or hill or be freestanding.

The prairie grasses had tough roots that were intertwined. Slabs of soil were held together tightly by these roots when cut. This allowed people to make bricks. Out of these tough, flexible slabs, settlers could build cheap, practical homes that were cool in summer and warm in winter.

Unfortunately, sod houses were not very comfortable or clean. Dust and earth constantly fell from the ceiling, which dripped mud when wet. Snakes and insects crawled out of the walls or dropped from the ceiling. Homeowners tried to combat these problems by tacking cloth over the ceiling or plastering the insides with whitewash and newspapers. Ceilings sometimes caved in if they were wet enough. Despite all of these annoyances, if you stood and gazed over the Minnesota prairies during the 1800s, you would see a field of flat grassy roofs as far as the horizon.

difficult. With the great distances and slow transportation, everyone knew they might never see each other again.

The wagons crossed the frozen river the first day of the trip. That night, as the two families rested at their camp, the ice broke. The families stayed in an abandoned cabin until spring, when traveling would be easier. When the trees grew new leaves, Charles, Caroline, and the girls said goodbye to Peter, Eliza, and the cousins. They headed west to Minnesota, where the treeless plains stretched as far as the horizon and the topsoil was deep. Charles told Mary and Laura the land was perfect wheat country—they would be rich!

Scandinavian Immigrants in Minnesota

While in Minnesota, the Ingalls family met many Scandinavian immigrants. People from Sweden, Denmark, and Norway started moving to the United States in the 1820s. By the 1870s, many had found their way to the Great Plains. The terrain there was suited to the farming life the immigrants were used to in their home countries. The influence of Scandinavian culture still can be found in Minnesota today.

In the spring of 1874, they pulled into the town of Walnut Grove, Minnesota. The little collection of plank buildings and muddy sidewalks was one of many towns that had sprung up along the new transcontinental railroad. Once again, the Ingalls family was part of the vanguard of settlement: Walnut Grove had been incorporated as a town only the previous year.

Charles went right to work. The family needed money and a place to live. He bought 172 acres (69 ha) from Anders Haraldsen, a Norwegian farmer. The place came with a dugout for the family to live in. Out on the prairie, housing supplies were scarce and expensive. All of the wood for houses had to be brought in by railroad. Haraldsen had done what practically every settler in the area had—he built a dwelling made of sod. He dug into the side of a creek bank and then built a wall across the front, with a hole cut into it for a door. The house was warm in winter, cool in summer, and extremely cheap to build.

Laura and Mary were fascinated. They had never lived in a house made of earth before. Also, their new house was right next to Plum Creek, which looked like a wonderful place to play. Water gurgled around rocks as colorful wildflowers and dragonflies danced in the wind and sun.

Everyone went to work immediately. Charles focused on cultivating the field, preparing to plant the wheat that would bring the family the money they desperately needed. While doing her many chores, Caroline continually battled the dust and earth that rained down from the ceiling and walls of her new house. Mary and Laura also had work. They were going to school for the first time. This was a big change for the sisters. They had never really been with groups of children their own age before. Laura was shy, but her travels had taught her not to be afraid of new experiences.

Laura quickly learned that she did not like simply doing what everyone else was doing. She had her own ideas about what games to play. Before long, she was the leader among the girls her age. One girl, however, did not want to play with Laura. Her name was Nellie Owens. Laura would always remember Nellie as a snobby, cruel girl who teased Mary and Laura for being poor and living in the country instead of in town.

At home, the Ingalls family was happy. Charles had plowed and planted a field of wheat that was growing beautifully. Mary and Laura played in the creek after school, brought the family cow home in the evenings, and helped their mother by watching baby Carrie. Charles was so sure of a successful harvest that he bought lumber and nails on credit. He built a lovely house on a little hill on the property that overlooked the old dugout in the creek bank.

Nellie Owens

Laura never forgot Nellie Owens, the girl in Walnut Grove who teased her. Laura wrote about Nellie, changing her name to Nellie Oleson and combining her with another snobby girl she encountered a little later in life named Genevieve Masters.

In the fall of 1874, when the wheat was standing heavy and tall in the fields, disaster struck Walnut Grove. An enormous invasion of grasshoppers descended in a cloud. There were millions of them. They covered everything: every house and every field.

The horde took only seconds to find the fields of ripe grain. Within a few days, the grasshoppers ate all of the wheat in the fields. Charles's crop was destroyed. He was counting on the wheat as currency to pay off the debt he owed on the building supplies.

Most of the neighbors were in the same predicament. Everyone tried to ward off the grasshoppers by keeping small smoky fires burning around their fields. Local officials even offered money for gallons of grasshoppers captured. It was useless. The grasshoppers ate everything: every leaf, every blade of grass, and every wildflower. The land was now dusty, brown, and covered with the insects.

Grasshopper Plagues

Giant infestations of grasshoppers, or locusts, were not uncommon in the Great Plains of North America. They still occur today in many parts of the world. In 2006, a cloud of grasshoppers descended on Cancun, Mexico, a popular resort town.

The Ingalls family was determined to have a farm on Plum Creek. Now that the wheat crop was destroyed, the family needed money to pay off its debt on the house and to buy seed to plant next year's crop. Charles

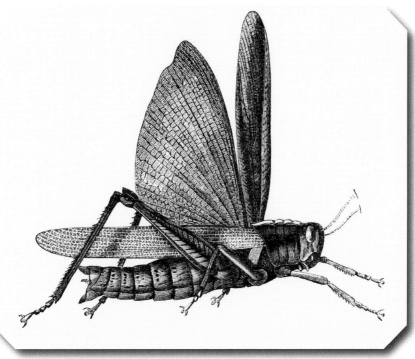

Grasshoppers destroyed crops in Walnut Grove, Minnesota, two years in a row. Without their crops for currency, life for the Ingalls family and their neighbors was difficult.

packed a small bundle, kissed his wife and daughters, and headed toward the eastern part of the state. The grasshoppers had not touched fields there, so laborers were needed to bring in the harvest.

Mary and Laura missed their father terribly while he was away, but being busy helped the time pass until Charles's return. Their days were filled with school, helping their mother, and playing with each other.

Caroline had the challenging tasks of caring for her three young children, running the household, and taking care of the livestock. She did all of this hard work alone and while pregnant.

One can only imagine the relief Caroline must have felt when Charles returned safely with enough money to carry the family until the next wheat crop. On November 1, 1875, the first Ingalls boy was born. He was named after his father: Charles Frederick. His doting sisters called him Freddie and carried him around like a doll.

The next planting season, Charles sowed a small field of wheat. There was none of the exuberant optimism of the previous year. Unfortunately, this crop would also not survive until harvest. Just as the first wheat sprouts showed green above the black earth, the grasshoppers returned. Once again, they took only a few days to eat everything back to brown, dusty, and ugly.

It was too much struggle and disappointment for the family. They failed to make a crop—their only source of income—for two seasons. With the new baby, Charles would not return to work the fields in the east as he had done the previous year. The family needed a fresh start. It was time to move again.

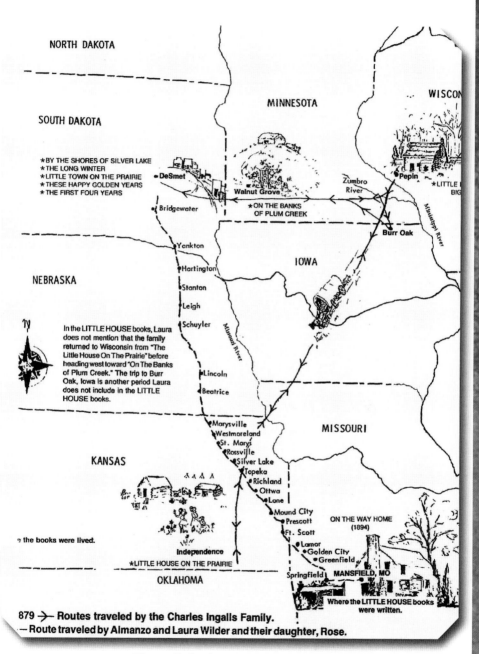

NORTH DAKOTA

MINNESOTA

WISCON

SOUTH DAKOTA

★BY THE SHORES OF SILVER LAKE
★THE LONG WINTER
★LITTLE TOWN ON THE PRAIRIE
★THESE HAPPY GOLDEN YEARS
★THE FIRST FOUR YEARS

●DeSmet

Walnut Grove

Zumbro River

●Pepin

★LITTLE
BIG

Mississippi River

●Bridgewater

★ON THE BANKS
OF PLUM CREEK

Burr Oak

●Yankton

IOWA

●Hartington

NEBRASKA

●Stanton

●Leigh

●Schuyler

In the LITTLE HOUSE books, Laura
does not mention that the family
returned to Wisconsin from "The
Little House On The Prairie" before
heading west toward "On The Banks
of Plum Creek." The trip to Burr
Oak, Iowa is another period Laura
does not include in the LITTLE
HOUSE books.

Missouri River

●Lincoln

●Beatrice

●Marysville
●Westmoreland
●St. Marys
●Rossville
●Silver Lake
●Topeka

MISSOURI

KANSAS

●Richland
●Ottwa
●Lane

●Mound City
●Prescott
●Ft. Scott

ON THE WAY HOME
(1894)

e the books were lived.

●Lamar
●Golden City
●Greenfield

Springfield

MANSFIELD, MO

Independence

★LITTLE HOUSE ON THE PRAIRIE

OKLAHOMA

Where the LITTLE HOUSE books
were written.

879 ➔ Routes traveled by the Charles Ingalls Family.
— Route traveled by Almanzo and Laura Wilder and their daughter, Rose.

*The Ingalls family settled in many different
areas throughout Laura's childhood and youth.*

Carrie, Mary, and Laura Ingalls

Hard Times

Though moving would bring the possibility of success, the Ingalls family must have felt sad as they packed the wagon and hitched up the horses yet again. No one wanted to leave their lovely little house on the hill near the bubbling creek. Even so, there was no future for them in Walnut Grove.

Friends of the family, the Steadmans, had purchased a small hotel in Burr Oak, Iowa, and invited Charles and Caroline to help run it. Mary and Laura could help, too. In return, the family would get room, board, and a small salary. Charles did not want to run a hotel. He wanted to farm on the open prairie. Caroline also did not want to run a hotel. She worried about the drinking and rough life the girls might see at the saloon on the first floor of the hotel.

The journey from Walnut Grove to Burr Oak was a gloomy one. Even baby Freddie, cooing in Caroline's arms, could not cheer up the family. They were back trailing—heading east instead of west. For pioneers, this meant failure. It was a disgrace that Charles felt keenly.

Laura was happy to be in the wagon again. She loved traveling and seeing new places. She was confident the family would be fine. Each night, they camped on the open prairie under the stars. They stopped at Peter and Eliza's farm on the Zumbro River, on the eastern side of Minnesota. Laura and Mary ran with their cousins in the meadows, ate plums that hung in thickets in the creek bottoms, and brought the cows home in the twilight. Charles and Caroline sat with Peter and Eliza in the evenings and talked quietly, wondering if they would be able to make enough money in Burr Oak

Two Teachers

Throughout her life, Laura vivdly remembered several schoolteachers. Two stood out particularly clearly. Will Reed was a gentle young man who taught the town school in Burr Oak. Laura adored him. Even in her old age, Laura remembered the speeches and poems he taught her. She credited him with sparking her life-long love of reading.

The other teacher could not have been more differ-ent. "Uncle" Sam Masters taught the school in Walnut Grove. Laura recalled him as very thin and old, with scraggly whiskers and bad breath. She wrote that Uncle Sam had a bad habit of putting his face very close to little girls when he talked to them. He would hold their hands. Laura hated him and did not want to hold his hand, so one day she held a pin between her fingers at school. When Uncle Sam squeezed Laura's hand, he got quite a surprise. He never tried to hold her hand again.

to support the family. Charles wondered if he would ever see the open prairie again.

After a few months, Charles and Caroline prepared to head to Iowa. They could not stay with Peter and Eliza any longer. The Steadmans were expecting them in Burr Oak. Before they could start out, something terrible happened that many pioneer families experienced: baby Freddie fell ill. No one knew what sickness he had. The doctor could do nothing for him. Freddie got increasingly sick until he died. He was only nine months old.

Cold rains fell during most of the trip to Iowa. The family silently endured the jolting wagon and creaking wheels. Each member thought both of Freddie and of the house and friends left behind in Walnut Grove. Laura was probably stunned. Her family had never had much money, but they always had joy and love. She was learning a hard, grown-up lesson: even when you love someone, they sometimes leave forever.

Laura would learn other lessons during her time in Burr Oak. She was nine years old and a sharp observer of other people's behavior. The Masters Hotel, where Charles and Caroline worked, was a fascinating place. Burr Oak was a quiet little town far from a river or rail line, but the hotel and its saloon always had plenty of activity. Men drank quarts of beer and whiskey late into the night and then shot each other in arguments over women and money. People were pushed through walls and thrown out onto the street. There was even a bullet hole in an interior door.

Fortunately, these activities did not reflect most of the boarders. The hotel residents were generally respectable people. Caroline cooked, cleaned, and did their laundry. Charles made repairs and tended to daily complaints and problems. Laura and Mary watched Tommy Steadman, a baby. They disliked watching Tommy because he cried all the time. Laura and Mary also had to play with Johnny Steadman. He was about

Infant Deaths

The death of baby Freddie devastated the Ingalls family. During the 1800s, almost every family had at least one child who died. The most common causes of death were typhoid, cholera, and yellow fever, diseases to which young children were particularly vulnerable.

their age and lame in one leg. Laura thought he was a loathsome boy. He was spoiled by his mother and would pinch girls and steal their toys. This was another lesson for Laura: she had to be kind to people who were not always kind in return.

As much as Laura and Mary liked the hotel and Burr Oak, Charles and Caroline did not. They did not like their girls being around the rough men in the saloon. They did not like waiting on guests. They wanted their own house. Charles in particular hated living in the heart of town. He thought it was dirty, noisy, and crowded. The family did not even have room for a cow of their own.

To make matters worse, Charles was barely making enough money to keep the family from poverty. He did a few odd jobs in

Bringing the Cows Home

In his book *Laura,* historian Donald Zochert records a particularly beautiful quote from Laura in which she describes one of her sweetest childhood memories:

Bringing home the cows is the childhood memory that oftenest recurs to me. ... I think it is because the mind of a child is peculiarly attuned to the beauties of nature and the voices of the wildwood and the impression they made was deep. I am sure old Mother Nature talked to me in all the languages she knew when, as a child, I loitered along the cow paths forgetful of milking time and stern parents waiting, while I gathered wild flowers, waded in the creek, watched the squirrels hastening to their homes in the treetops and listened to the sleepy twittering of the birds.[1]

addition to working at the hotel. He took a partnership in a flour mill and did carpentry around town, but still it was not enough. As his girls grew tall and strong, Charles became thin. His face was creased with lines. His shoulders became bent with strain and sadness.

Although Charles and Caroline were not happy with their living situation, they had joy. The birth of their fifth child was cause for celebration. Grace Pearl was born in 1877. She had golden hair and bright blue eyes. Her arrival caused worry as well because she was another mouth to feed, but Grace was a welcome gift of life after Freddie's death.

In addition to Grace's arrival, another change was in store. After two years in Burr Oak, the family had as little money as when they arrived. They were in debt. Charles desperately wanted to get back to farming and leave the crowded town. The family had heard from friends that the grasshoppers had left Walnut Grove. Perhaps they should try again. Surely, things could not be any worse in Minnesota than they were in Iowa.

Painful Times

When Laura created the Little House books, she chose not to write about Burr Oak and the return to Walnut Grove. She felt Freddie's death and Charles's inability to find steady work would be too painful for her readers.

In 1878, the Ingalls family's covered wagon rolled out of Burr Oak. Charles was jubilant—they were headed west, back to the open prairie. Throughout the journey, Charles played his fiddle as Laura, Mary, and Carrie danced around the campfire.

Charles, Caroline, Laura, and her sisters were welcomed back to Walnut Grove by their many friends. Their house on the hill was owned by someone else now, but Charles built another little house at the edge of town. He still did not have enough money for a farm, so he opened a small butcher shop for a time, did more carpentry, and even made brooms.

Laura was now ten years old. She was old enough to realize how much the family needed money. Laura knew she had to help. She ran errands for neighbors and cared for their children. She even took care of a woman who was sick. Before long, Laura had a reputation in town as being a reliable girl. For a time, she waited tables in the hotel in town. Caroline reluctantly allowed Laura to miss school in order to work. This was a sign of just how much the family needed the money Laura earned.

Growing Up Quickly

Laura was doing the work of a woman by the time she was ten years old. In pioneer days, girls were expected to grow up fast. Their mothers depended on them to help with chores and to care for younger children.

Pioneer girls usually helped with the work in their own homes, and sometimes performed work for other families, too.

Even with Laura's hard work and added income, the Ingalls family could not get out of poverty.

The family also could not avoid tragic events. In the spring of 1879, Mary suddenly became seriously ill. She had a high fever and sharp pains in her head. She was delirious for days. Later, doctors told the family Mary had suffered a stroke. Caroline, Charles, and the doctor gathered around Mary's bed. They waited anxiously to see what would happen. Laura kept Carrie and Grace quiet and out of the way. Everyone feared Mary would die.

Mary did not die. She slowly got better. As she grew stronger, however, something happened. Mary's eyesight deteriorated. She was going blind. Dr. Jacob Wellcome, a surgeon, came by train to examine Mary. He told the family the nerves in Mary's eyes had been damaged by the stroke and that there was nothing he could do. Finally, Mary was strong enough to sit up in a rocking chair padded with pillows. The last thing she ever saw, Laura wrote later, was the bright blue of Grace's eyes as she stood gazing up at Mary.

Mary Ingalls went blind after the nerves in her eyes were damaged by a stroke.

The town of De Smet, South Dakota, circa 1880

A Prairie Homestead

Mary's blindness spurred Laura's growing up. Laura was now like the oldest girl. She was only 12, but Laura needed to act more grown up. Charles and Caroline depended on Laura to help care for her younger sisters. Laura longed to run, jump, and roll in the grass as she

did when she was little. Instead, she had to help Mary
and Caroline—it was her duty to the family.

Charles sometimes stood at the door of the little
house, gazing down the road for long periods of time.
He wondered where they would get enough money
for a farm. Where could they go?

One day, the answer came up the road wearing
a brown sunbonnet and driving a fine bay horse.
It was Docia, Charles's sister. She had
come all the way from the Big Woods.

Docia explained that she married
a man who was in charge of the gangs
building the new transcontinental
railroad, which ran through Walnut
Grove. The railroad was eventually
going to run all the way to California,
but right now the lines were being
laid in Dakota Territory. Docia's
husband needed a good man to
go out to the railroad camp and
be a bookkeeper.

Charles's face lit up. He knew
immediately what this meant. The
government had been offering
homesteads free to any settler who

The Great Dakota Boom

The period of 1878 to 1886
was the Great Dakota Land
Boom. After a long period
of economic depression,
railroad building began
again during this time.
More than 2,000 miles
(3,218 km) of rails were
laid. The railroad brought
people to the area. South
Dakota's population more
than tripled during the
boom. In 1888, settlers
pushed for statehood.
Passed in 1889, the En-
abling Act separated the territory into the Dakotas and
gave statehood to South
Dakota. Pierre was made
the capital.

would agree to live on the land for five years and plow it for crops. After that, the land was given to the settler. If Charles, Caroline, and the girls went with Docia, Charles could make enough money to get the family started on a claim and pay for the journey.

Though she did not yet know it, this move would be one of the great adventures of Laura's life. The family became part of the Great Dakota Boom, a rush for settlement that came as huge areas of untouched land were made accessible by the new railroad. Gangs of men sang across the prairies, swinging picks as they laid the shining rails.

The Homestead Act

Like most people in Dakota Territory during the late 1800s, the Ingalls family benefited from the Homestead Act of 1862. The federal government wanted to settle the land it obtained in the Louisiana Purchase. Congress passed a law stating that any man or woman who was an American citizen could file on and claim a 160-acre (65 ha) plot in a certain area of the West, including Dakota Territory. The settler had to agree to live and work on the land for at least five years or buy the entire claim outright for $1.25.

As Laura wrote in *By the Shores of Silver Lake*, in which she describes the family's experience establishing a homestead, competition for land was fierce. Plots near the rail lines, like the one the Ingalls family claimed, were in high demand. Despite the massive influx of pioneers, less than half actually made it through the required five years. Many of the people who came out had little or no experience farming. Many could not tolerate the isolation and primitive living conditions of the prairies. Those who persevered—like Charles and Caroline Ingalls— usually spent the rest of their lives on their claims.

On their heels, all along the lines, people rushed to claim land. Settlers were eager to build houses and stores and to farm the land.

Laura once more found herself heading west while perched on the wagon seat, the rough prairie wind blowing against her face. It was her favorite place to be.

The Ingalls family arrived at a location with no name. Prairies surrounded them for miles. Clouds of dust rose like smoke as the shouts of the railroad gangs and the clang of metal sounded. It was an untamed place, but Laura loved the wild, rough land and the wild, rough gangs of men living and working on it. The family moved into a tiny shanty near the railroad camp. Charles quickly went to work for the railroad company.

Caroline worried about the influence of the uncivilized railroad camp and workers on her girls, so she kept Laura and her sisters close to home. Laura studied her schoolbooks and helped with housework.

Turnips

Laura sometimes felt parts of her life were too difficult for children to read about. When she wrote her books about homesteading, *By the Shores of Silver Lake* and *The Long Winter,* she chose not to describe how hungry the family was during their first year in De Smet. She remembered her father leaving the table still hungry so that the family could have more, and then seeing him eat raw turnips straight from the fields. Turnips were the only food the family had plenty of.

When she drew water from the well, Laura would gaze over the empty prairie and take deep breaths of the sweet, clean air. She was content.

One day, Charles came home excited. The family had been offered a wonderful opportunity. The railroad gangs would pack up and head back East once the cold weather set in. The bosses asked if Charles and his family could stay at the deserted camp during winter to watch over the railroad company's equipment. They could live in the house the surveyors used—a fine frame house stocked with plenty of food. Charles would be able to scout the nearby land for the perfect claim spot and be first in line at the land office when it opened in the spring to file on the land.

The family accepted the offer to stay at the railroad camp. The winter was uneventful. The weather was so mild that the family ate New Year's dinner with the door open, reveling in their solitude in the cozy house on the empty prairie.

When spring came, Charles went to the land office in the town of Brookings and filed on his claim of land. He had expected to be first in line, but Charles was actually almost too late. At the first sign of snowmelt, homesteaders started pouring into the country to fight for claims. A town was springing up near the railroad camp: a printer, a grocer, a mailman, and a barkeeper had already settled.

The work on the family's claim was hard the first year. Charles quickly built a tiny shanty, but its one room was drafty and cramped. Plowing the tough prairie was difficult and endless work for both people and horses. Also, there would be no more money until there was a crop, which would not come until next year's harvest.

By now, there was an actual town on the prairie: De Smet. It had a Main Street, two grocers, a furniture store, a railroad depot, and a telegraph station. Early on, Charles built a store on a lot that he had hoped to eventually rent out to a tenant. The family soon moved to the store to spend the winter. They had no idea it would be one of the hardest winters of their lives.

The winter of 1880 was knownfor many decades afterward as the "Hard Winter." That year, the Dakotas experienced seven months of blinding blizzards and bone-chilling

George and Maggie Masters

The Ingalls family was not alone during the Hard Winter. A young couple lived with the family. George and Maggie Masters had a new baby. Charles and Caroline took the couple in out of pity. They were terrible guests who were greedy and unhelpful. Laura disliked them so much that when she wrote the story about the Hard Winter, she chose to leave them out.

The Ingalls family stayed in the surveyor's house during the winter to guard the railroad camp until spring, when the workers would return.

cold. The blizzards arose suddenly, at any time of the day or night. The storms were deadly to anyone caught in them. Unable to see, people would wander until they froze to death. There was no choice but to stay inside, huddled close to the stoves, trying to stay warm. The storms dumped so much icy snow on the rail lines that the trains could not get through. No trains meant there would be no supplies, including coal and food. Everyone did their best to conserve. Before long, people had to twist hay into sticks to burn. Some people started eating their precious seed wheat—their only hope for a crop in the spring. Others had planned on buying their seed right before planting time in the spring. Those families had almost nothing.

Though difficult to imagine, the Ingalls family was in a situation worse than a lot of other people because they had fewer supplies than many other families. Many settlers in De Smet were in their first year there. Settlers usually brought supplies with them, so the first-year settlers likely had more than the Ingalls family, who were in their second year. Every day, Laura and her family ground the little wheat they had in their coffee grinder. Caroline would make a small loaf of unleavened bread. All the while, everyone twisted hay into sticks as fast as they could, so they would have enough heat to keep the family from freezing.

Everyone was growing desperate—and winter was only half over. A young homesteader named Almanzo Wilder and his friend, Cap Garland, had heard that

The Long Winter

Laura wanted to call her novel of the winter of 1880 *The Hard Winter,* which was how all the settlers referred to that season. To avoid making the book seem hard or difficult, her publishers suggested a title change. They and Laura agreed on *The Long Winter.*

a homesteader 12 miles (19 km) out of town had a supply of wheat. If someone could reach him and get some of that wheat, the settlers in De Smet would have enough food to survive the winter.

Despite the danger of blizzards, Wilder and Garland drove across the open prairie in the terrible winter weather to find the settler. This was something no one else in town had dared to do. Their bravery saved the town from starvation. For the rest of their lives, old folks in De Smet would remind each other of the Hard Winter and the young men who risked their lives to get that wheat.

A stagecoach fights the blizzard during the Hard Winter.

Laura Ingalls at 17

A Prairie Girl Grows Up

pring brought trains and new life to De Smet. After the Hard Winter, many settlers gave up pioneer life and returned home. Even so, De Smet continued to grow. For every one family who left, three new families arrived. The newcomers were enthusiastic about the little town. They had a lot

of news and ideas from relatives in cities back East.
De Smet boomed. The town boasted two newspapers,
an ice cream parlor, several hotels, multiple grocers,
druggists, lawyers, bankers, and merchants of every
kind. There was even a roller-skating rink.

Laura did not spend much time in town. Like the
rest of the homesteaders, the family moved back out
to their claim as soon as the first snowmelt arrived.
They worked sunrise to sunset to create a producing
farm. Charles planted the fields with potatoes, corn,
wheat, and turnips. Caroline and the girls cooked three
times a day, cleaned the house, made clothes, and took
care of their new flock of chickens. Laura helped
Caroline plant a magnificent garden with a variety of
vegetables. Laura's favorite chore was milking the cows
in the morning and evening. She would sit with her
head pressed against a warm flank, her feet wet with
dew, inhaling the sweet bovine fragrance.

The spring and summer after the Hard Winter flew
by. No one really saw their neighbors much during the
planting season because everyone was so busy working.
After the fall harvest, the Ingalls family moved back to
town so Laura and Carrie could return to school.

Laura was a young woman now. Her assertive
personality was showing. She demanded fairness

from everyone around her. She refused to partake in snobbery, though she did like to be attractive. Laura was pretty, with beautiful blue eyes. She liked to wear fashionable clothes.

Eliza Jane Wilder

The first fall after the Hard Winter, Eliza Jane Wilder, Almanzo's sister, was the teacher in De Smet's school. Laura wrote about her in *Little Town on the Prairie*. Miss Wilder was one of the first authority figures with whom Laura did not get along. Laura thought Miss Wilder disliked her, played favorites in school, and was mean to Carrie. Laura wrote that Miss Wilder was unable to control the children who rebelled against her and refused to study.

Despite her shortcomings as a teacher, Eliza Jane Wilder was a strong and independent woman. She was 31 and single when Laura met her. She had moved to the West with her brothers and filed a claim of her own. Miss Wilder farmed her own crops and took care of her parents in Minnesota. Later, she worked at the Department of the Interior in Washington, D.C. She married a man 18 years older who had six children. She took care of them and had a child of her own. Laura and Almanzo would eventually send their own daughter, Rose, to live with her independent-minded Aunt Eliza. Rose grew up to be a strong-willed career woman herself and credited Eliza Jane with influencing her in that regard.

Her liveliness made Laura quite popular among her classmates. They had a good time together during school recess. They were all old enough now to start noticing each other as more than playmates. Several boys asked Laura out on dates—to go walking or to dances. She was not interested in these boys. She was waiting for another boy to ask her out: Cap Garland.

Laura thought he had the loveliest white-blond hair she had ever seen.

Laura was also gaining a reputation in town as a scholar. She excelled in her studies, especially writing, reading, and history. Caroline had always insisted that her daughters keep up with their studies, even when the family was far from a school. It seemed

Prairie Schools

The Bouchie schoolhouse where Laura taught had one room heated by a wood-burning stove. She had five students. This was common for Western settlement schools at the time.

natural to Laura to study hard and enjoy learning. She impressed the local school board by reciting a lengthy oral history of the United States at a school exhibition. In 1882, she was offered a contract to teach at a school 12 miles (19 km) south of town, even though she was one year younger than the legal limit for teaching.

This was Laura's first real job. It was also her first time away from her family. She was only 15 years old and not very tall. She would likely be younger and smaller than some of her students. In addition, the school was too far for Charles to get Laura on the weekends. She would not be able to go home until the end of the eight-week term.

In the settlements that dotted the prairie, residents typically banded together to build a small schoolhouse.

Morgan Horses

Almanzo drove two brown Morgan horses when he picked up Laura at school. The Morgan is a smaller horse known for its strong, arched neck and pretty head. Almanzo was very fond of the breed and owned at least one Morgan his entire life.

They would hire a teacher, and one family would provide her room and board. The family boarding Laura was Louis Bouchie, his wife, and their little boy. Laura was homesick the moment Charles left her at the Bouchie family's door, but matters were much worse once Laura met Mrs. Bouchie. The woman was cold and rude to Laura. Mrs. Bouchie made it clear that Laura was not welcome. She hated the West and everything about it. The house was sloppy and dirty. Mr. and Mrs. Bouchie quarreled every night. One night, Laura woke to see Mrs. Bouchie standing in the bedroom holding a butcher's knife. Whether she was going to kill or injure herself, her husband, or Laura is not clear, but it did not matter. Laura was petrified and miserable living with the family.

To make matters worse, the winter was terribly cold. Cracks in the schoolhouse walls were so big the snow blew through them and drifted in piles on the floor. Three of Laura's five students were indeed both bigger and older than she, so Laura had trouble controlling them. Laura did not give up or complain. She had not come all the way out to the Dakota prairies and lived through troubles such as grasshoppers and blizzards only to be scared by her students.

The eight weeks were not all bad. Thanks to Almanzo Wilder, Laura was able to go home every weekend. Every Friday, Almanzo picked up Laura from the schoolhouse in his new handmade cutter pulled by his beautiful brown Morgan horses. Laura knew Almanzo only as the man who had saved the town by getting the wheat during the Hard Winter. He was a full ten years older than Laura—25 to her 15.

Laura loved going home, but not necessarily with Almanzo. She knew why he was willing to drive so far every week in the bitter cold. She was not sure she liked it. Laura thought if Almanzo was interested in her, then she must be honest with him. Laura told Almanzo straight out that she was not interested in him romantically. She was only going with him so she could get home.

Manly and Bess

Laura frequently told a story about getting to know Almanzo. On one long drive, the question came up of what they should call each other. Almanzo said his brother called him Mannie, but Laura misheard Almanzo say, "Manly." When Laura realized her mistake, she said she thought Manly was a nicer nickname anyway. Almanzo said he already had a sister Laura and never really liked the name. Laura told him her middle name was Elizabeth, a nickname for which is Bess. For the rest of their lives, Laura and Almanzo called each other Manly and Bess.

Age at Marriage

Laura was always self-conscious about the age gap between herself and Almanzo. She had no reason to be concerned. On the frontier at that time, most husbands were four to nine years older than their wives.

This news did not deter Almanzo one bit. He liked Laura and had his eye on her for a wife.

When the school term ended, Laura returned to town. Not everything was the same in her life. Now there was Almanzo. He did not disappear once school ended. As soon as the snow melted, he started calling on Sundays in his new buggy. Almanzo and Laura would go on long drives for miles around the lakes and sloughs, talking all the while. They laughed and sang together.

Laura and Almanzo found their personalities well-suited to one another. He was a quiet, slow speaker who preferred to listen. She was talkative and lively. He liked her independent spirit and strong-willed ways. She liked his reliability, his quiet self-assurance, and his skill with his beautiful horses. Charles and Caroline also liked Almanzo. He was a steady man with a good reputation. He had a claim and was a good farmer. He treated Laura well. After three years of courtship, Laura and Almanzo married August 25, 1885. She was 18 and he was 28.

*Almanzo at age 28 and
Laura at age 18, the year
they married*

Laura and Almanzo Wilder shortly after they were married

Joy and Heartbreak

*L*aura and Almanzo Wilder were filled with
hope for their new life together. Almanzo
built a beautiful little house for Laura that she loved.
It was like all of the other little houses she had lived in
throughout her life, except this house was better in one
special way—it had Almanzo in it.

Laura and Almanzo knew making their homestead produce enough to live on would be hard, but they were young and strong. Almanzo tended the fields. He bought expensive machinery on credit to help with the wheat and oats. He was not worried about going into debt. The crops looked spectacular. The debt would be paid off after the harvest.

Laura sometimes helped Almanzo in the fields, even driving six horses hitched to a binder. Mostly, she took care of house chores. Doing the housework alone was very different than doing it with her mother and sisters. Laura never liked washing, sewing, and cooking. Now a wife, she had to do it all by herself. She often felt lonely and worried about money.

Laura was surprised to find that Almanzo had a lot of debt. There was a mortgage on the claim, the livestock, all the farm machinery, and on the materials used to build the house.

This debt was only the beginning of the troubles Laura and Almanzo would experience. The first years of their marriage would be some of the most difficult years of their lives.

Rhubarb Pies

Laura used to tell a story about one of the first meals she cooked as a bride. The threshers were helping Almanzo bring in the harvest. To please the group of hungry men, she baked rhubarb pies. Unfortunately, she forgot to add sugar. Rhubarb is extremely sour. She served the pies to the threshers, who were very polite about it.

The crops that first year, 1888, did not produce the money needed to pay off Almanzo's debts. There was no chance to harvest them because a hailstorm flattened the wheat field one week before threshing was to begin. The entire crop was lost. Fortunately, Almanzo was able to harvest the oats. The little bit of money from that crop paid the interest on a few debts and bought groceries for a year.

Many more problems followed. First, the barn and haystacks burned down. Then, both Almanzo and Laura came down with diphtheria, a

Their First Four Years Together

When Laura wrote the stories of her childhood in the Little House novels, she meant to stop at the point of her marriage to Almanzo, the story told in *These Happy Golden Years*. Many years later, long after Laura and Rose had both died, a manuscript about Laura and Almanzo's first four years of marriage was found among Rose's things. Laura only wrote a rough draft. No one really knows why. Perhaps she lost interest in publishing after Almanzo died. Roger Lea MacBride, Rose's lawyer and long-time friend, edited the manuscript and published it under Laura's name.

The book stands out because its terse, spare style is very different from the dramatic, descriptive prose of Laura's other books. The events in the book are very sad: loss, grief, sickness, and death. Some scholars speculate that Laura intended the book for adults.

Laura always wrote from the perspective of the child or teenager Laura in her books. The problem she encountered with the *First Four Years* was that now there was an adult Laura. The book had to be written from that perspective, so it really would not be a children's book. Laura struggled with this idea as she wrote the manuscript, but she never left any explanation for the book.

common but dangerous illness.
The doctor visited them several
times, which was an added expense
they would have to pay. Almanzo
suffered a slight stroke during
his recovery, which made him lose
some use of his hands and feet.
He could not work at the same
pace anymore—just when the
couple desperately needed the
profits from the farm. A drought
began that burned up the crops for two years in a row.
There was no money at all to pay the debts.

Diphtheria

Diphtheria is an infectious disease in which a bacteria poisons the body. People suffering from diptheria have difficulty breathing, a high fever, and weakness. There is also a risk for damage to the heart and central nervous system.

The final two blows came during the fourth year
of Laura and Almanzo's marriage. These proved to be
almost unbearable. In 1889, Laura gave birth to a baby
boy who looked just like Almanzo. He died when he was
only 12 days old, before Laura had a chance to name
him. Less than two weeks later, their house burned
down. Laura and Almanzo were able to save only a few
dishes and clothes. Everything else was destroyed.

Through all of the hardships, there was one thing
that kept Laura and Almanzo from despair: their
daughter, Rose. Born December 9, 1886, she was
a beautiful little girl with bright blue eyes like her

The grave of Laura and Almanzo's unnamed son, who died 12 days after birth

mother's. As the crops withered in the fields and her father struggled to hitch the horses with his shaking hands, Rose grew fat and happy. She would be Laura and Almanzo's only child.

In 1890, Laura and Almanzo were heartsick and worn out. So were other farmers in the area, which was gripped by an economic depression and a major drought. Crops withered and the soil turned to dust. The Wilders felt desperate. There was no money and they could hold off their creditors no longer. They had only managed one small harvest in four years. That was it. They decided to leave.

The Wilders wandered the next
four years in search of a place to
rebuild their lives. They traveled
to Spring Valley, Minnesota, to
stay with Almanzo's parents. They
could not afford a place of their
own in Minnesota. Next, they
moved to Florida. Since his stroke,
the harsh winters of the Dakotas and
Minnesota affected Almanzo greatly.
The warm climate might be easier on him.

Death of the Baby Boy

Laura and Almanzo's baby
boy died of convulsions,
but no one ever knew why.
The baby boy, who was
never named, is buried in
De Smet, along with
Charles, Caroline, and Mary
Ingalls.

Laura had never been to the South before, so the
panhandle of Florida was as odd a place as she had ever
seen. Alligators barked at night in the swamps around
their little farm. The Spanish moss hung like ghostly
arms from the oak trees. The air was thick and heavy.
The heat made Laura sick. Neighbors stared at her in
silence. She carried a gun for protection. Laura was
terribly homesick for clear blue skies and the fresh
prairie winds. Florida was simply too different. After
a year, the Wilders headed north.

Laura was saddened by De Smet when they returned.
The town was still suffering from economic depression.
Many farmers had moved. Her parents were growing
old. Charles was beginning to suffer the effects of the

heart disease that would eventually kill him. He could not work the land as he used to, so he and Caroline rented out the claim and moved into town with Mary, Carrie, and Grace.

Laura and Almanzo knew that farm life could be heartbreaking. An easier time could be had in town, but they wanted to grow crops, raise animals, and be independent. Laura and Almanzo longed for their own place. They bought a house a block from Charles and Caroline. While Rose went to school, Laura sewed buttonholes 13 hours a day for a dressmaker. Almanzo worked any job he could find. The couple saved every dollar they could.

Laura and Almanzo knew they were not going to stay in De Smet, but they were not sure where they would go next. One day, Almanzo brought home a brochure titled "The Land of the Big Red Apple." Breathlessly, he and Laura read about the Missouri Ozarks, a place neither of them had ever been before. ⟶

Give Us This Day

One of the few things Laura was able to save from the fire that burned down the Wilders' house was a bread plate from the Montgomery Ward catalog. The plate was glass. Around the edge it was inscribed with "Give Us This Day Our Daily Bread." Laura kept the plate her entire life. It is now on display in the Laura Ingalls Wilder Museum in Mansfield, Missouri.

After reading about the Ozarks in the brochure "The Land of the Big Red Apple,"
Laura and Almanzo Wilder moved to Missouri.

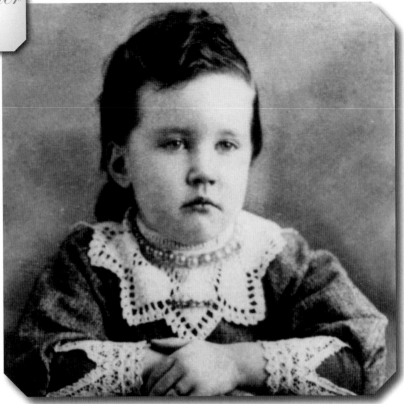

Rose Wilder, Laura and Almanzo's daughter

A HOME AT ROCKY RIDGE

*L*aura and Almanzo survived tremendous hardship in the first few years of their marriage. They were young and strong. When she felt hopeless, Laura sometimes would talk about giving up farming and opening a store in town, but she was never really serious. She and Almanzo knew they would not be happy any place where they could not see the sun rise over their own fields.

It was 1894. The country was still in a terrible economic depression. The unemployment rate was 10 percent. Laura and Almanzo had a wagon, a $100 bill, and a young daughter. The brochure about the Land of the Big Red Apple prompted them in a new direction—they were going to Missouri to find a farm! The trip would be long. Laura knew she would probably never see her family again.

Laura rode next to Almanzo in the wagon, with Rose tucked behind them. Down through Nebraska they went, and through the corner of Kansas. The temperature soared to 110 degrees Fahrenheit (43° C). They met encampments of Russian immigrants who gave them gifts of freshly baked bread. As the Wilders traveled south, the terrain changed from the flat land with black soil of the prairie to rolling foothills with rocks. They drove up the Ozark Mountains. Higher and higher the carriage climbed until Laura, Almanzo, and Rose reached the town of Mansfield, Missouri. This was it—the Land of the Big Red Apple they had read about. The brochure was right—everywhere, as far as the eye could see, there were apple orchards bursting with red and gold fruit. There were more than apples. There were peaches, plums, blackberries, and cherries. Laura thought the land was going to be great for farming.

With their $100 bill, Laura and Almanzo put a down payment on 40 acres (16 ha) of land. It was uncleared, full of pine seedlings, brush, and rocks. The only shelter on the property was a rough log cabin. This would be their home. The land had great potential, but it needed a lot of work. It also needed a name. They called it Rocky Ridge Farm.

The House at Rocky Ridge

By the time Almanzo finished working on the farmhouse at Rocky Ridge, it had become something of a local showpiece. The house had ten rooms, picture windows, built-in bookshelves, and a stone fireplace. Almanzo built the house using materials almost entirely from the property.

The family moved into the log cabin on the property. Rose went to school. Laura and Almanzo set to work. They cut down trees, pulled stumps from the ground, and pried up hundreds of limestone rocks from the fields. Using the wood from the trees he and Laura cut down and the rocks they cleared, Almanzo built a one-room shanty near the log cabin. Later, he added on a room, and then another. More fields were cleared and crops were planted. The crops were harvested. Almanzo built a beautiful rock fireplace in the house.

Laura started a flock of Leghorn chickens. Laura and Almanzo got to know their neighbors.

The years slowly passed: plowing time, planting time, harvesting time. The trees turned all shades of red, gold, and purple in the fall. Every morning, Laura got up before dawn and went to her favorite ridge on the farm to watch the sun rise.

Rose became a brilliant student. She had long read every book in the school library. She loved learning, but Rose was not happy. She did not like the farm life— the endless milking, weeding, and cooking. Rose was smart and frequently felt that she was somehow more special than the other children in her school. She longed to see the faraway places she had read about in books. The people Rose saw around her in Mansfield seemed so dull and narrow-minded because they were consumed with farming matters that did not interest her, such as the price of grain and if the cows were making good milk.

More than anything, Rose hated being poor. The Wilders had food, clothes, and their house, but money was always tight. The family depended on the success of the crops and livestock. If the crops failed, they might lose their farm or not have enough money to buy the things they needed. Rose hated having to wear old clothes and not being able to buy the things that children in town had. By the time she was a teenager, Rose was ready to leave Missouri. When Aunt Eliza Jane visited, she invited Rose to live with her in Louisiana, where Rose could attend a big-town high school. Laura and Almanzo must have worried about letting their only child go at such a young age, but they knew Rose was unhappy. After much discussion, Rose packed her bags and headed for Louisiana by train with her aunt.

Laura and Almanzo bought more land every year until they had about 160 acres (64 ha). Almanzo had long finished the house. It was now sprawling and peaceful on the hill overlooking the

The Ozarks

The Ozark region is a rocky, hilly area that covers about half of the state of Missouri and some of Arkansas. The Ozarks are not true mountains. They are a plateau with sunken valleys. The land is known for its natural beauty. Rolling hills covered with oak, elm, maple, and pine trees are interrupted by rushing rivers and waterfalls. The Osage tribe once lived in the hills. This was the tribe Laura met as a little girl in Kansas. When Laura met them, the Osages had been pushed west off their Ozark homeland by the United States Army.

The original European settlers of the Ozarks were of Scotch-Irish descent, similar to those who settled the Appalachian Mountains. The area was isolated, so a distinct Ozark culture has developed through the centuries. People from the area tend to have distinct accents, slang words, and cultural activities. Today, the Ozark region relies heavily on tourism to supplement the agricultural economy.

fields. Laura baked bread, kneading the dough as she looked out the windows. She cared for her flock of chickens. Almanzo tended the crops and raised his beloved Morgan horses.

The Writing Wage

Laura received $5–$10 per article for her column in the *Missouri Ruralist.* That is equivalent to $100–$200 now.

Now entering middle age, Laura still had lots of energy. She joined several farm women's clubs, which offered social outlets for the often isolated women on Ozark farms. She served as the local loan officer for the Federal Land Bank for 12 years. Her expertise in raising her chickens and increasing their egg production was known throughout the community, so she was frequently invited to give talks on poultry to the farm clubs. One day, Laura was unable to attend a meeting, so she sent her speech to be read by someone else. That talk on chickens was the start of her writing career.

John Case, editor of the *Missouri Ruralist,* was in the audience of the farm club that day. He liked Laura's descriptive prose and clear convictions. He invited her to write a piece about farming life for the statewide farm publication. Laura could not have been more surprised. She had never written for money, but Laura was always interested in anything new, so she told the editor she would try it.

Laura's first article for the *Missouri Ruralist* appeared February 18, 1911. "Favors the Small Farm Home" was written under the name "Mrs. A.J. Wilder." The readers loved her theme of families working together and preserving the traditional ways of farming. The editors asked her for another piece. Soon, Laura was writing regularly for the paper, although she sometimes published under Almanzo's name. No one really knows why she did this—perhaps she thought readers would take a man more seriously than a woman. Eventually, the paper offered Laura a regular column, "As a Farm Woman Thinks." In her column, Laura offered farm wives a variety of farming tips, beauty hints, and housekeeping advice.

While Laura was starting her writing career, Rose was off having adventures. She was an innovative and unconventional woman for her time. When she was only 19, Rose moved, eventually landing in San Francisco, California. She lived

The Good Farm Wife

In an article for the *Missouri Ruralist*, Laura writes that a good farm wife "must know her own business, which includes the greatest variety of trades and occupations ever combined in one all-around person. Think of them! Cook, baker, seamstress, laundrywoman, nurse, chambermaid, and nurse girl."[1]

*In her column, "As a Farm Woman Thinks," Laura Ingalls Wilder offered farm
wives a variety of farming tips, beauty hints, and housekeeping advice.*

alone there. She became a telegraph operator, which
was one of the few occupations other than teaching
a single young woman could do respectably. Like her
mother, Rose became a writer. She started writing
for newspapers on the West Coast and soon became

a full-time journalist. Rose also became a novelist. She gained a respectable literary reputation and was quite popular with the fashionable crowd of New York City.

As an adult, Rose traveled to the faraway places she had always dreamed about visiting: Tirana, Albania; Constantinople (modern-day Istanbul), Turkey; Cairo, Egypt; Paris, France; Beirut, Lebanon; and Baghdad, Persia (modern-day Iraq). The life Rose lived was very different from the quiet life on Rocky Ridge Farm.

Rose's Travels

Rose visited many faraway places on her travels, but she wanted to travel more. She was frustrated that she did not travel around the world. She was preparing to go on a world cruise when she died.

Rose Wilder during her traveling days

The house Almanzo built on Rocky Ridge Farm

LITTLE HOUSE
COMES TO LIFE

t the beginning of the 1930s, Laura
was Mrs. A.J. Wilder, a small-town
farm wife who sometimes wrote for a newspaper. Most
of the time, she did chores at home. She sewed, tended
chickens, and baked pies. By the mid-1940s, she was

Laura Ingalls Wilder, a popular children's writer on her way to becoming one of the best-selling children's authors of all time.

Laura never had any intention of writing novels. She and Almanzo had a pleasant life on Rocky Ridge Farm. They were proud of the home they made together, but money was always tight. The possibility of poverty was never far away. Nationwide, the Great Depression was setting in. People everywhere were struggling to survive. Laura worried constantly about their bills, and once had the electricity turned off to save money.

Rose returned to the United States in 1923. She traveled between New York, where she had an apartment, and her parents' home. Whenever she was in Missouri, Rose felt trapped. She knew her parents had little money saved. As the only child, she would have to support her parents in their old age—something she did not want to do. Rose wanted to travel. She wanted to write undisturbed. Rose hated everything to do with small-town life.

Early Reviews

Critics loved Laura's books. Anne T. Eaton of the *New York Times Book Review* wrote of Laura's work, "[Memories] of pioneer life are described with zest and humor. The characters are very much alive and the portrait of Laura's father, especially, is drawn with loving care and reality."[2]

Rose had already made a successful career for herself as a writer, so she thought her mother could make some money writing. She encouraged Laura to turn some of her memories of growing up on the prairies into stories, and then into a novel. *Little House in the Big Woods*, Laura's first published book, was an instant sensation. Laura's editors at Harper and Brothers wanted more manuscripts. Laura quickly turned out the rest of the *Little House* series, eventually writing eight published books.

The period during which Laura wrote was a difficult one for Americans. The Great Depression and

---

Novels or Memoirs?

Most people assume Laura's books were autobiographies, but she said from the beginning they were not—they were novels, works of fiction. Of course, the books are mostly true. All of the events Laura wrote about actually happened to her and her family. All of the characters really existed. To make the stories easier to understand, multiple people from Laura's past were sometimes combined into one character. Sometimes people were completely left out. If she portrayed someone in an unflattering way, Laura usually changed the person's name so as not to upset them.

Places and times were occasionally rearranged to simplify the stories. For example, the Ingalls family actually left the Big Woods twice, returning to the cabin from Kansas before leaving for Minnesota. Laura skipped that part in her books. She wrote that the family went straight to Walnut Grove from Kansas.

Another big change Laura made was advancing her age in *Little House on the Prairie*. In reality, she was only a baby when the family moved to Kansas. She was too young to remember anything. In order to allow the little girl Laura to tell the story from her own perspective, Laura and Rose made her several years older.

World War II made people eager for entertainment that took them away from the troubles of poverty and war. Laura's tales of horses, log cabins, and her father's fiddle were what readers craved.

Recommended Reading

The 1932 edition of *The Bookman's Guide to Gift Books for Young People* recommended Laura's first book, *Little House in the Big Woods,* stating, "Laura Ingalls Wilder recalls her own pioneer childhood of nearly 60 years ago. Life on the edge of the Big Woods of Wisconsin— making bread, seeing bear tracks in the snow, going to town, getting a new calico dress, hearing wolves howl—becomes a romance for twentieth-century girls."[1]

Once she was a published author, Laura's life quickly changed. She started traveling at the request of her publishers. She went to schools, libraries, and book fairs all over the country. Children lined up for her autograph and to tell Laura how much they loved her books. She was asked to give speeches about writing. Her mailbox overflowed with fan letters—bags and bags every day! The town of Mansfield was overwhelmed because their own Mrs. Wilder was a famous author.

Laura's success was not hers alone. Many people never realized that Rose helped Laura with most of the Little House books. Laura had never written a full-length book before she started *Little House in the Big Woods,* but Rose had experience writing a novel. Rose showed her mother how to make descriptions lively and set the pace of a novel. After Laura wrote a chapter, Rose would edit it.

She would smooth out her mother's words, change sentences around, or add dialogue. Eventually, Rose edited all of Laura's books.

Some scholars and historians have argued about how much Rose did to Laura's books. Some people have questioned who really authored the stories. Some have said Rose was the true author and Laura provided the material. Some have said Rose did not really do anything at all, Laura did it mostly herself. It is likely that Rose was Laura's personal editor. Laura thought of the stories and wrote all the parts of the books: the scenes, the characters, and the dialogue. Rose helped Laura fine-tune her writing by making suggestions to improve the books. Sometimes Laura took Rose's suggestions; sometimes she did not.

Despite her fame, Laura's life did not change much. She still lived at Rocky Ridge Farm with Almanzo. She still got up every morning to watch the sun rise. She still baked her own bread—and she still hated kneading it. One thing was different: money. For the first time in their lives, Laura and Almanzo had plenty of money. They did not have to worry about bills or debt anymore. They even bought a car.

When Laura finished her last novel, *These Happy Golden Years,* in 1943, she was 76 years old. By that time, libraries had been named after her. Five of her eight books were runners-up for the top award for children's books, the Newbery Medal. The Association of Library Services even created a special award in Laura's name. The Laura Ingalls Wilder Award is given annually to an author who has made a lasting contribution to children's literature.

Though she was successful, Laura was growing tired. Her family had long died. Charles, Caroline, Mary, Carrie, and Grace were all gone. Laura was the last Ingalls. She still traveled some and made speeches, but Laura simply wanted to stay home with Almanzo. He still plowed a little every year, but Almanzo was slowing down. Almanzo died in 1949. He was 92.

After Almanzo's death, Laura did not have much interest in her fame as an author, even though her books were more popular than ever. She missed Almanzo terribly. The farm felt big and lonely without her partner of more than 60 years. Rose was in New York and rarely came home. People from the community drove Laura around and helped with her chores. She grew frail with age. Laura died February 10, 1957. She had just turned 90.

In some ways, Laura traveled a long journey from the little cabin in the Big Woods where she was born. She was part of the great westward expansion of the United States. She saw Native Americans leave their homelands forever. She lived through blizzards, grasshopper plagues, and fires. She witnessed the deaths of her brother and son. With Almanzo, she created a successful farm and raised a successful daughter. She wrote eight books that were enjoyed and loved by countless readers.

In other ways, Laura never stopped being a pioneer— on the prairies, on her farm, or in her words. She never lost her outspokenness, her bravery in the face of challenge, or her strong sense of right and wrong.

A Place to Rest

Laura is buried next to Almanzo in the cemetery in Mansfield, Missouri.

Laura Ingalls Wilder lives on today in the pages of her books and in the hearts and minds of her readers. Her books are among the top 60 best-selling children's books in the history of publishing. More than 45 million copies have been sold worldwide. No one can say exactly what these books have meant to their countless readers. Laura's depictions of a simple life lived with a strong and loving family still touch people today. ⌐

Laura Ingalls Wilder signing books in her late seventies

TIMELINE

1867	1869	1870
Laura Elizabeth Ingalls is born February 7 in the "Big Woods" of Wisconsin.	The Ingalls family arrives in Independence, Kansas, in September.	The Ingalls family returns to the Big Woods.

1879	1885	1886
The Ingalls family moves to De Smet, South Dakota.	Laura Ingalls marries Almanzo Wilder in De Smet August 25.	Rose Wilder is born December 9.

1874

The Ingalls family arrives in Walnut Grove, Minnesota, in August.

1876

The Ingalls family moves to Burr Oak, Iowa.

1878

The Ingalls family returns to Walnut Grove in January.

1889

Laura's baby boy dies in August, 12 days after birth.

1890

The Wilders move to Westville, Florida.

1892

The Wilders return to De Smet.

TIMELINE

1894	1932	1933
The Wilders move to and purchase land in Mansfield, Missouri.	*Little House in the Big Woods* is published.	*Farmer Boy* is published.

1940	1941	1943
The Long Winter is published.	*Little Town on the Prairie* is published.	*These Happy Golden Years* is published.

1935	**1937**	**1939**
Little House on the Prairie is published.	*On the Banks of Plum Creek* is published.	*By the Shores of Silver Lake* is published.

1949	**1957**	**1968**
Almanzo Wilder dies October 23.	**Laura Ingalls Wilder dies February 10.**	**Rose Wilder dies October 30.**

ESSENTIAL FACTS

Date of Birth
February 7, 1867

Place of Birth
The "Big Woods" of Wisconsin

Date of Death
February 10, 1957

Place of Death
Mansfield, Missouri

Parents
Charles and Caroline Ingalls

Education
High school

Marriage
Almanzo Wilder, August 25, 1885

Children
Rose Wilder, and one unnamed son who died 12 days after birth.

Career Highlights
Worked as a teacher when she was only 15, which was one year younger than the legal starting age.

Started her writing career as a columnist for a statewide newspaper, the *Missouri Ruralist,* offering farm women farming tips, beauty hints, and housekeeping advice.

Published eight children's books that have sold millions of copies.

Societal Contribution
Laura Ingalls Wilder's Little House books have entertained countless readers worldwide.

Residences
Moved throughout the Midwest as a child and as an adult. Lived in Florida with her husband and daughter for about one year.

Quote
"Children today could not have a childhood like mine in the Big Woods of Wisconsin, but they could learn of it and hear the stories Pa used to tell. But I put off writing them from year to year and was past 60 when I wrote my first book, *The Little House in the Big Woods.*" —Laura Ingalls Wilder

ADDITIONAL RESOURCES

SELECT BIBLIOGRAPHY

Harmon, Melissa Burdick. "Laura Ingalls Wilder: Her Real Life on the Prairie." *Biography*, August 2001: 88–93.

Holtz, William V. *The Ghost in the Little House: A Life of Rose Wilder Lane*. Columbia, MO: University of Missouri Press, 1993.

Miller, John E. *Becoming Laura Ingalls Wilder: The Woman behind the Legend*. Columbia, MO: University of Missouri Press, 1998.

Miller, John E. *Laura Ingalls Wilder's Little Town: Where History and Literature Meet*. Lawrence, KS: University Press of Kansas, 1994.

Romines, Ann. *Constructing the Little House: Gender, Culture, and Laura Ingalls Wilder*. Amherst, MA: University of Massachusetts Press, 1997.

Spaeth, Janet. *Laura Ingalls Wilder*. Boston: Twayne Publishers, 1987.

Wilder, Laura Ingalls. "Notes from the Real Little House on the Prairie." *Saturday Evening Post*, September 1978: 56–57, 104–105.

Zochert, Donald. *Laura: The Life of Laura Ingalls Wilder*. New York: Avon Books, 1976.

FURTHER READING

Anderson, William. *The Little House Guidebook*. New York: HarperTrophy, 2002.

Lasky, Kathryn C. *Searching for Laura Ingalls Wilder*. New York: Aladdin, 1998.

Stine, Megan. *The Story of Laura Ingalls Wilder: Pioneer Girl*. New York: Bantam Doubleday Dell Books for Young Readers, 1992.

Wilder, Laura Ingalls. *A Little House Traveler: Writings from Laura Ingalls Wilder's Journeys Across America*. New York: HarperCollins, 2006.

Web Links

To learn more about Laura Ingalls Wilder, visit ABDO Publishing Company on the World Wide Web at **www.abdopublishing.com.** Web sites about Laura Ingalls Wilder are featured on our Book Links page. These links are routinely monitored and updated to provide the most current information available.

Places to Visit

Laura Ingalls Wilder Historic Home and Museum
3608 Highway A, Mansfield, MO 65704
417-924-3626, 800-924-7126, www.lauraingallswilderhome.com
Tour Rocky Ridge Farm, which has been preserved exactly as Laura left it at the time of her death.

The Laura Ingalls Wilder Memorial Society
P.O. Box 426, De Smet, SD 57231
800-880-3383
www.liwms.com
This organization offers tours of various Ingalls and Wilder sites, provides information about the families, and displays some of their artifacts.

Laura Ingalls Wilder Museum
330 8th Street, Walnut Grove, MN 56180
800-528-7280
www.walnutgrove.org/museum.htm
See items from the Ingalls family and memorabilia from some of the stars from the *Little House on the Prairie* television series.

Laura Ingalls Wilder Park and Museum
3603 236th Ave., Burr Oak, IA 52101
563-735-5916
www.lauraingallswilder.us
Visit one of Laura's childhood homes, which is now a nationally recognized landmark. Also, tour the Masters Hotel and other places in the town Laura and her family frequented.

Glossary

bookkeeper
> The person responsible for keeping and recording the accounts for a business.

cutter
> A light sleigh made to carry one or two people.

debt
> Something owed.

delirious
> Suffering from confusion, inattention, and oftentimes jumbled speech and hallucinations.

depression
> A period of extreme economic decline in which business activity and prices decrease and unemployment increases.

dugout
> A shelter formed by a pit dug into the ground or the side of a hill.

fiddle
> The common name for a violin.

grassland
> An area of land, such as a prairie, that has grass or grasslike vegetation.

habitat
> The environment in which an animal usually lives.

homestead
> The land claimed by a settler.

icon
> A person who has become well-respected and admired, usually for their work in a particular field.

insulation
> Protection from the outside, particularly wind, rain, snow, and extreme temperatures.

intrigue
> To create interest or desire in.

jubilant
> Extremely happy or joyful.

memoir
> The story of the experiences of the author.

migration
> The movement of many people or animals from one place to another.

plumb
> To examine in detail.

prose
> The ordinary language used in writing and speaking; not poetry.

reservation
> A section of land set aside for a particular purpose, such as for Native Americans to live.

saloon
> A place where alcohol is sold and drunk; a bar.

salt pork
> Fatty pig meat that has been soaked in salt water to keep it from spoiling.

scalplock
> A style in which a long piece of hair is left on the top of the head and the rest of the skull is shaved bald.

shanty
> A small, crude cabin or shack.

slough
> A swampy area with deep mud and long grass.

sod
> Grass-covered soil held together by matted roots.

stroke
> A sudden loss of brain function as the result of blood vessel blockage or rupture; it can cause brain damage and loss of function.

surveyor
> A person whose job it is to measure the elevation and boundaries of land.

vanguard
> The leading position in a movement.

vignette
> A short descriptive literary account.

vulnerable
> Susceptible to physical or emotional harm.

Source Notes

Chapter 1. The Book No Depression Could Stop

1. John E. Miller. *Becoming Laura Ingalls Wilder: The Woman Behind the Legend.* Columbia, MO: University of Missouri Press, 1998. 186.

2. Donald Zochert. *Laura: The Life of Laura Ingalls Wilder.* New York: Avon Books, 1976. 227.

3. Laura Ingalls Wilder. "Notes from the Real Little House on the Prairie." *The Saturday Evening Post,* September 1978: 56.

Chapter 2. Born in the Deep Woods

1. Donald Zochert. *Laura: The Life of Laura Ingalls Wilder.* New York: Avon Books, 1976. 19.

Chapter 3. Discovering the Prairie

1. Laura Ingalls Wilder. "Notes from the Real Little House on the Prairie." *Saturday Evening Post,* September 1978: 56.

Chapter 4. Adventures on Plum Creek

None.

Chapter 5. Hard Times

1. Donald Zochert. *Laura: The Life of Laura Ingalls Wilder.* New York: Avon Books, 1976. 96.

Chapter 6. A Prairie Homestead

None.

Chapter 7. A Prairie Girl Grows Up

None.

Chapter 8. Joy and Heartbreak

None.

Chapter 9. A Home at Rocky Ridge

1. Laura Ingalls Wilder. *Missouri Ruralist,* 5 August 1919. Qtd. in Miller, John E., *Becoming Laura Ingalls Wilder: The Woman Behind the Legend.* Columbia, MO: University of Missouri Press, 1998. 136.

Chapter 10. The Little House Comes to Life

1. Nancy Evans. "The Day of Days Is Here!" *The Bookman's Guide to Gift Books for Young People,* December 1932: 847.

2. Anne T. Eaton. Rev. of Little House in the Big Woods, by Laura Ingalls Wilder. *New York Times Book Review,* 24 April, 1932: 9.

INDEX

INDEX CONTINUED

ABOUT THE AUTHOR

Emma Carlson Berne has a master's degree in composition and rhetoric from Miami University in Oxford, Ohio, and a bachelor's degree in English from the University of Wisconsin–Madison. She has written and edited many books for children and teenagers, including biographies of Christopher Columbus and the rapper Snoop Dogg. Emma lives in Charleston, South Carolina, with her husband, Aaron, and her parakeet, Avital.

PHOTO CREDITS

Laura Ingalls Wilder Memorial Society, De Smet, S.D., cover, 3, 13, 16, 42, 52, 58, 62, 95, 96 (top), 97 (bottom), 99; Hoover Presidential Library and Museum, 6, 11, 51, 69 (top), 87, 88, 98; Courtesy of Laura Ingalls Wilder Home Association Mansfield, MO, 15, 31 (bottom), 41, 70, 78, 96 (bottom); North Wind Picture Archives, 23, 24, 32, 39, 49, 61, 85, 97 (top); Photo Courtesy of the South Dakota State Historical Society-State Archives, 31 (top), 69 (bottom); Deb Houdek Rule, www.dahoudek.com, 74; Ryan Beyer/Getty Images, 77